For

Craig

When I think of Paris, I think of you.

Elegance

Elegance

The Beauty of French Fashion

Megan Hess

Hardie Grant

BOOKS

Contents

Introduction

F rench fashion is all in the details. It is delicate, understated and demure – you only need look at a classic Chanel suit and its woven wool tweed made in France or, if you can get close to one, run your fingers over the soft leather of an Hermès Birkin bag. The masters of French fashion do not rely on excess, instead approaching design with simple elegance.

In my career as a fashion illustrator I have always been drawn to French haute couture, but I was sketching the famed looks of Chanel, Dior and Saint Laurent long before it became my livelihood. I first experienced French fashion as a little girl, when I was mesmerised by Audrey Hepburn's effervescent Holly Golightly. It was while repeatedly watching *Breakfast At Tiffany's* that I became familiar with Golightly's simple yet glamorous wardrobe. The way she wore her little black dress and string of pearls instantly struck a chord with me, and I remember drawing my own version of her outfits in my little sketchbook.

Until this point in my young life I had never thought to find out who designed the clothes I thought so beautiful. But now I needed to know who was responsible for such fashion mastery, and I came across a French designer named Hubert de Givenchy. It was at this moment that my love of French fashion was born.

The ten designers featured in this book have had an enormous impact on me as a woman and on the way I see the wonderful world of fashion. I have selected my favourite looks from recent collections and a special few from decades past, hoping to highlight the stories of these designers that are so loved today.

One of the reasons I love French fashion is because it's slow and focused. Sometimes in this busy world we need to be reminded that beauty cannot be rushed. The original style of many French designers has remained intact since their beginnings.

Hermès, the oldest designer featured in this book, started selling leather horseriding accessories some 180 years ago, and the house is now home to the most recognised handbag in the world – the Birkin – keeping the link to leather at the forefront of everything they do. The cinched waists and full circle skirts of Dior's New Look, which debuted in the 1940s, are still referenced in collections today; the same is true for Chloé's enigmatic, whimsical style, first seen over breakfast and croissants at Paris's famous Café de Flore in 1956.

But French fashion also has the ability to adapt with the times, with a new wave of designers who have reinvented these heritage labels. Karl Lagerfeld led Chanel creatively from 1983 until his death in 2019, while Marc Jacobs was the first designer to introduce wearable fashion into Louis Vuitton's long leather history in 1997, and Phoebe Philo was responsible for dressing the modern French woman during her decade at the helm of Celine.

Intermingling the new with the old has kept French fashion perpetually in demand, and from that mix we have seen classic designs perfected over decades. I love how nearly all French fashion houses have their signature piece that so uniquely represents them. For Saint Laurent, it's the famous tuxedo suit jacket; for Hermès, the silk scarf; and for Louis Vuitton, the iconic monogrammed travel trunk.

French fashion has also led a revolution in the way we dress and interact with fashion every day. It gave us *prêt-à-porter* clothing: Chloé founder Gaby Aghion believed fashion should be accessible to all and made her clothing ready-to-wear, removing the exclusivity of haute couture. French fashion taught us that style does not have to come at the expense of comfort: Coco Chanel was the first to move away from the corseted and restrictive styles of her era, instead designing liberated, looser fitting garments made from jersey and tweed. Meanwhile, Hubert de Givenchy offered women choice with his 1952 debut range of separates: in a time when a woman's wardrobe largely comprised dresses, this allowed women to pick and choose what they wanted to wear based on comfort, style and personal taste.

French fashion is wearable art, and the city that inspires it is the canvas. Over the years I have been fortunate to visit Paris many times for my work. I love everything about the fashion capital. It is one of those rare cities that you can enjoy to its fullest no matter what you are doing. Paris makes the ordinary extraordinary: from a freshly baked baguette wrapped in beautiful paper to a corner store that will box your single macaron with a silk ribbon, even the simplest tasks are completed with grace.

During Paris Fashion Week, I often think of the overwhelming contributions to style that French designers have made. It's not so much the women on the runways, but the women in the audience that remind me of the importance of French fashion. Whether attending a show, on their busy morning commute, or inspecting seasonal vegetables at the market, Parisian women are always dressed impeccably. For those who have grown up surrounded by French fashion, style is effortless.

Fashion should be a joy, not a chore. French designers show us that innate style comes from within: you must dress yourself for your self. It's a simple philosophy, but that's what makes it so perfect.

'Simplicity is the keynote of all true elegance.'

– Coco Chanel

01

Chanel

I t's no secret that I love Coco Chanel – I've already written an entire book about her colourful Parisian life. Her revolutionary designs changed the way women dressed forever, while her rags-to-riches story goes to show that with hard work anything is possible.

Coco Chanel's resilience and determination to forge ahead in life was a product of her difficult childhood. Born Gabrielle Bonheur Chanel in 1883 in Saumur, a town in western France, Chanel faced a series of hardships in early life. Her parents struggled to make ends meet and provide for their family, and this only intensified when Chanel's mother passed away in 1895. Her widowed father made the heartbreaking decision to send twelve-year-old Chanel and her sisters to an orphanage run by nuns in central France, hoping a better life awaited them there.

This turned out to be the most fortuitous event in Chanel's life: at the orphanage the nuns taught her to sew. The intricacies of hand-sewing ignited her interest in fashion and self-sufficiency, and would later inspire her in the foundation of the Chanel empire.

On leaving the orphanage, Chanel found a job as a seamstress, but also moonlighted as a cafe singer. It was at the cafe that Chanel acquired the nickname Coco, and left behind her difficult past as Gabrielle. A new name presented the opportunity for a new beginning. Chanel became the centre of a flourishing social scene, befriending the cafe's upper-class patrons. However, realising she lacked the voice to become a professional singer, she decided to stick with the one thing she knew how to do well: sew.

In 1910 Chanel opened a millinery boutique on rue Cambon. She sold her hats to the wealthy women she had befriended in

'Dress shabbily and they remember the dress; dress impeccably and they remember the woman.'

– Coco Chanel

her cafe days. Her business was a success, and she opened a second boutique in Deauville in 1913 using money borrowed from her lover at the time, Arthur 'Boy' Capel. In 1915, Chanel again expanded, opening a third boutique in Biarritz, and was able to repay the entirety of Capel's original loan.

One of Chanel's first clothing designs, a jersey dress, was the result of necessity – she was shivering on a chilly trip to Deauville in Normandy and needed something warm to wear. The design was simple and chic, and repurposed jersey fabric traditionally used for undergarments. Here was a dress that defied the traditional and restrictive women's fashion silhouette with its stretch fabric and fluidity. It was groundbreaking, and Chanel's clients began requesting similar liberating looks. The popularity of the jersey dress prompted Chanel to step away from millinery and instead focus on women's clothing, a decision that would prove to be very wise.

By the 1920s Chanel was worth millions and had almost 2000 employees working in her atelier. She famously said of her wealth, 'My fortune is built on that old jersey that I'd put on because it was cold in Deauville.'

In the decade that followed, Chanel was able to manifest a timeless look that is still worn and referenced today. Her designs offered a new style of haute couture – a style that allowed women to embrace their independence and dress for themselves. The Chanel look was elegant yet refined, simple yet detailed, comfortable yet classic.

Chanel brought straight lines to the forefront of fashion at a time when over-the-top frou-frou looks reigned. She transformed black – a colour typically worn during periods of mourning – into a covetable wardrobe staple with instant chic appeal. She invented casual elegance with her striped Breton top, inspired by her travels to the French coast. She gave women power through her most iconic looks, the Chanel suit (a collarless tweed jacket with pencil skirt), borrowing from traditional men's silhouettes. She even gave fashion its most-loved item: the little black dress, a look that has not left the runways since the 1920s and featured in the Chanel Fall 2017 Couture collection (appropriately in tweed). She encouraged women to complete their understated looks with bold costume jewellery – in particular lots and lots of pearls.

Coco Chanel had come a long way from Gabrielle Bonheur Chanel, but it nearly all came undone following a series of scandals during World War II. Chanel closed her boutiques in 1939 and embarked on an affair with a German officer during Germany's occupation of France. By the end of the war her name was tarnished and she was forced to move to Switzerland.

After more than a decade of quiet reflection, Chanel returned to Paris – and to fashion – in 1954. Reopening her atelier at age seventy, Chanel introduced more of her famous looks to market, with bellbottom pants, braid-trimmed cardigan jackets and two-tone monochromatic heels. She worked up until her death at eighty-seven in 1971.

The years immediately following Chanel's passing saw the introduction of the label's first *prêt-à-porter* (ready-to-wear) range, in 1978. However, the most significant event of Chanel's new era must have been when businessman Alain Wertheimer assumed control and began looking for a new designer to inject vitality into the brand. His eyes were set on German designer Karl Lagerfeld. Wertheimer persuaded Lagerfeld to leave his design post at Chloé and join Chanel as creative director in 1983.

Even though Coco Chanel never met her successor, the spirit of the label remains due to Lagerfeld's incredible ability to honour her original designs and breathe new life into them. Looking to the past when designing for the future is what Lagerfeld did best. Many of my favourite Lagerfeld looks from the Pre-Fall 2015 collection reference the heritage of the Chanel label and specifically the famous Chanel suit: I especially love the monochromatic nod to the two-piece suit with its chevron leather trim.

When I heard the sad news of Karl's passing, I was so shocked – somehow I thought he would live forever because he was just so iconic. On that day, I posted one of my favourite illustrations of all time: Karl in a Chanel hot air balloon soaring high above the Paris skyline. I like to imagine that Karl and Coco are now finally together, both dressed in their tweed Chanel threads.

While Chanel is synonymous with black, the first designer handbag I ever bought was in fact a pink Chanel 2.55. I was beginning my career as a fashion illustrator and with every commission I put aside a little bit of money towards the classic quilted bag. It motivated me to keep on illustrating, and finally after a year of saving, I was able to walk into a Chanel boutique to proudly purchase it.

Coco Chanel innovated women's fashion forever with her ability to fuse comfort and style. She is so woven into fashion history that it would be impossible to image it without her. The house continues to take its responsibility to dress women seriously – generation after generation with simple elegance.

CHANEL

CHANEL

CHANEL

CHANEL

02

Dior

Christian Dior was a superstitious man. Before a fashion show he would consult his tarot reader, sew a sprig of his favourite flower – lily-of-the-valley – into the hem of his runway looks, and name a coat in each collection after his hometown of Granville. He took every measure to ensure his collections would be met with success, but to me the greatest contribution to his success was not his assortment of good luck talismans but his pure talent.

Dior's creativity manifested in various entrepreneurial pursuits in his early life before eventually finding its place in fashion. Born in 1905 on the coast of Normandy to wealthy parents, Dior was one of five children. In 1910 his family relocated to Paris, a city he instantly connected with. While Dior's parents had hopes he would become a diplomat, they quickly realised their son's talents were pointing in a different direction: the world of fine art.

Financed by his father, Dior opened a gallery that enjoyed much commercial success and even sold the works of his friend Pablo Picasso. Things were moving steadily for Dior until the Great Depression hit and devastation touched the Dior family – his mother and brother died, and a few years later his father's business collapsed. The tragic events forced the closure of Dior's flourishing gallery and initiated a turning point in his career.

Forced to create a new path for himself, Dior started selling fashion sketches on the street. His drawings landed him a job illustrating fashions for *Figaro* magazine, which led to him becoming a design assistant at Robert Piguet, where he worked until he was conscripted for military service.

'Elegance must be the right combination of distinction, naturalness, care and simplicity.'

– Christian Dior

Returning to Paris after his army duties, Dior worked at fashion house Lucien Lelong alongside a fellow emerging designer poised for similar success, Pierre Balmain. Balmain suggested they go into business together but Dior declined. Perhaps he knew his big break was just around the corner.

That break came when Dior was approached by Marcel Boussac, who owned several factories that had been left empty post–World War II. Boussac offered the factories to Dior to start his eponymous label. Unlike some of the fashion wunderkinds in this book who dived into fashion at a young age, Dior was forty-one when he opened his business in 1946; I find that so inspiring. He had the courage to steer his life in a completely different direction and take a chance on himself.

Dior debuted his first collection of ninety looks in 1947 to critical acclaim. One of his earliest supporters was *Harper's Bazaar*'s then-editor Carmel Snow, who famously called the collection the 'New Look'. This moniker swept the press and left a lasting impression – even today Christian Dior is known as the founder of the New Look.

Dior was a pioneer of post–World War II fashion, masterminding a new style of opulent and extravagant dressing. His designs not only contrasted with the simple straight-line garments of Chanel, but were also in direct opposition to postwar fabric restrictions. Dior's new look was defined by tailored gowns with cinched waistlines and full skirts – some using metres and metres of voluminous tulle. His Bar jacket (a double-breasted blazer with a cinched waist) and accompanying A-line circle skirt was a novel style for a generation of women looking to reclaim femininity (it's also

wrong!

one of my personal favourite looks). Dior reignited a spark in French haute couture that had been snuffed out during the war. His garments brought light and glamour back into women's wardrobes.

Dior's lasting influence on the shape of French fashion didn't end there. He also designed the H-line silhouette, which controversially fell just below the knee; the tulip silhouette, inspired by his time gardening in his hometown of Granville; and the Junon dress, which featured individual petal-shaped fabric pieces covered in embroidery and jewels. Dior became known for his lavish designs and would make made-to-measure clothing for his clients, many of whom would travel internationally to be fitted in his atelier.

Dior tragically died of a heart attack in 1957 – just a decade after starting his label. His unexpected death came at the height of the label's popularity and the world was looking for someone to honour the Dior legacy. That someone came in the form of Dior's precocious protégé Yves Saint Laurent, who was only twenty-one at the time.

Under intense pressure from his fashion peers and the media around the world, Saint Laurent knew that his first collection as creative director had to be perfect. There was no room for error. In 1958 Saint Laurent launched his Trapeze collection, focusing on looser silhouettes with slim shoulders and swinging skirts: the New Look for a new generation.

Since then Dior's successors have continued to reference the late couturier's extravagant elegance while still leaving their own distinguished mark on the house. Following from Saint Laurent was Marc Bohan with his 'slim look' silhouette,

> '**A dress is a piece of ephemeral architecture, designed to enhance the proportions of the female body.**'
>
> – Christian Dior

then Gianfranco Ferré with his architectural style, and then John Galliano, who guided the house of Dior into the new millennium and paved the way for Raf Simons. For Simons' critically acclaimed debut collection for Dior – Fall 2012 Couture – strapless gowns in hues of soft pink littered the runway in an homage to the dresses of the original New Look. Simons' journey to creating this first collection was captured in the fascinating documentary *Dior and I*.

The ultimate feminine brand now finally has its first female creative director, Maria Grazia Chiuri. Her most recent collections incorporate Dior's classic feminine shapes – such as her silk version of the Bar jacket (2019 Resort) – and edgily pair past and present, with Dior T-shirts emblazoned with feminist slogans and tough biker boots (Spring 2019 Ready-to-Wear).

How the past merges with the present is something I wanted to capture when I was invited to live-sketch Dior's couture runway show in London in 2017. Illustrating the looks as they moved down the runway was magical, but having the opportunity to draw some of the women attending the show in head-to-toe Dior couture was even more rewarding, because Dior's clothes are made to be worn and enjoyed. The real fashion shows are always off the runway.

I think it's remarkable that even though Christian Dior only ran his business for a decade, those following in his footsteps have stayed true to his original sense of style. New looks are born and worn every day but the New Look is in a class of its own, and Dior will always be known for being the man who brought it to the world.

03

Saint Laurent

Yves Saint Laurent is French haute couture's most famous prodigy. At just twenty-one – an age when most people spend their time studying, travelling, socialising and figuring out which path to take in life – Saint Laurent was announced as creative director of Dior. The year was 1957 and shortly afterwards, in 1961, he would go on to start his own haute couture house, working until he retired in 2002. For Yves Saint Laurent there really was no choice: fashion was always going to be his destiny.

Born in 1936 in Algeria, Saint Laurent came from a wealthy family; his father was a local businessman, a lawyer by trade who also owned cinemas. Saint Laurent, however, struggled to find his place. Shy, introverted and demure, he was often the subject of ridicule by his classmates. He found solace in fashion, where he could express himself without the judgement of others. Saint Laurent spent his time creating paper dolls and eventually took his miniature designs life size when he started designing and making clothing for his mother and two younger sisters.

His parents were impressed with his talents and used their connections to arrange for him to be introduced to the editor of French *Vogue*, Michel de Brunhoff. He was equally impressed and encouraged Saint Laurent to move to Paris to study fashion. Saint Laurent enrolled in the Chambre Syndicale de la Couture at age eighteen, and his designs quickly attracted attention. Gaining confidence, he entered his sketches in an emerging fashion designer contest organised by the International Wool Secretariat, which he won. He entered the competition a second

'Fashion dies, but style remains.'

– Yves Saint Laurent

time and won again in the dress category, the same year that a young Karl Lagerfeld won in the coat category.

Saint Laurent's boy-genius reputation led to an introduction to Christian Dior via de Brunhoff. Legend has it that Dior hired Saint Laurent on the spot, and Dior went on to mentor his talented new young designer until Dior's unexpected death just a few years later, in 1957.

As per Dior's wishes, Saint Laurent succeeded him as head of the house of Dior. Saint Laurent's first collection afforded him international recognition – but while he had the freedom to experiment as creative director, this came at a cost. His looks became too removed from classic Dior silhouettes so when he was called up for compulsory military service, the house took the opportunity to replace him.

Devastated by this decision, Saint Laurent transformed his heartache into creative ambition. With the help of his business and life partner, Pierre Bergé, he started his eponymous label, Yves Saint Laurent, in 1961.

The new decade marked a new beginning for Saint Laurent. He took his experience and firsthand knowledge of Dior's New Look and reinterpreted it for the countercultural generation. Yves Saint Laurent became a fashion house synonymous with a fresh outlook on elegance. Borrowing from silhouettes of the 1920s, 1930s and 1940s, Yves Saint Laurent's designs were loosely fitted with shortened hemlines for liberated women who valued style and comfort.

Saint Laurent's signature looks include the revolutionary 'Le Smoking' suit: one of the first tuxedo jackets specifically designed for women. I remember when I was a young girl reading in my much-loved fashion magazines that every woman needs one great white shirt and one great tuxedo jacket to see her wardrobe through the years. I decided that one day I was going to own these investment pieces, and a few years ago my childhood dream became a reality when I purchased a Saint Laurent tuxedo jacket. There's something about the tailoring of the jacket that makes me feel incredible when I wear it, particularly over a white shirt. The shape, the cut, the fit ... everything is perfect.

While Le Smoking suit has become synonymous with the house, other recognisable styles also emerged in the mod era of the 1960s. Saint Laurent pioneered the beatnik look with jumpsuits, turtlenecks and trapeze swinging shift dresses, and brought androgynous looks for women into the mainstream. The black vinyl trench coat he designed for the Saint Laurent Rive Gauche collection in 1966 became iconic after being worn by French actress Catherine Deneuve in the film *Belle de Jour*.

Saint Laurent also interwove culture with fashion and was one of the first designers to use fine art in his work with his famous Mondrian collection, a series of six dresses inspired by the works of Piet Mondrian.

A modern businessman, Saint Laurent was an early adopter of *prêt-à-porter* fashion after he observed its success at Chloé in the 1950s. Traditionally, haute couture was reserved for the elite and wealthy, who would attend fittings and have their clothing made to order. Ready-to-wear offered customers a new ease; they could simply buy off the rack. It seems strange that there was a time where you could not walk into a shop in

> 'Isn't elegance
> forgetting what one
> is wearing?'
>
> – Yves Saint Laurent

the afternoon and buy a new dress for a party that evening, because ready-to-wear is what we have always known, and we have French fashion to thank for that.

As Saint Laurent grew older, new creative directors took the helm. Alber Elbaz had a brief stint before Tom Ford's tenure from 1999 to 2004. Ford is credited with bringing Yves Saint Laurent into the twenty-first century with his sophisticated looks and runway glamour borrowing from Saint Laurent's early collections.

Nearly a decade later the creative baton was passed from Ford to Hedi Slimane, who most famously dropped 'Yves' from the front of the house's name, and moved its headquarters from Paris to Los Angeles. Slimane's grunge and street aesthetic had mass appeal within youth culture and is largely responsible for the house's present-day popularity. His Spring 2013 Ready-to-Wear collection introduced Le Smoking suit into the new millennium, using the original style but cropping the blazer and giving it extra attitude by pairing it with knee-high patent leather boots and an oversized pussy bow.

Anthony Vaccarello leads the house today and continues to uphold Saint Laurent's legacy. His Spring 2018 Ready-to-Wear collection featured quirky silhouettes and very short hemlines that Saint Laurent would be proud of. While Saint Laurent learned his craft from the masterful Dior, his own liberated, edgy designs were a complete departure from restrictive, corseted garments. He was a true visionary.

SAINT LAURENT
PARIS

Spring
2018

Ready-to-
Wear

SAINT LAURENT
PARIS

Spring
2013

Ready-to-
wear

04

Lanvin

A s a working mother of two wonderful children, I often look to Jeanne Lanvin for inspiration in life and business. One of the nineteenth century's most successful couturiers and entrepreneurs, Lanvin's drive to create was born from her devotion to her daughter, Marguerite. The intrinsic bond of the Lanvin women still serves as a guiding light for the label today, 130 years after the house began.

Jeanne Lanvin was a pioneering and independent businesswoman – which might sound like many impressive women in your life, but was unfortunately rare in the early nineteenth century. Women were typically homemakers, but Jeanne sought a different path for herself.

Growing up as the eldest of eleven siblings, young Lanvin was nicknamed 'Little Bus': instead of catching the bus to school she would make her own way there, so she could save the fare for her future. A natural seamstress, Lanvin became a millinery apprentice when she was sixteen years old. At twenty-two, using the money she had saved from her wage (and all those bus fares), she opened her own millinery boutique in Paris with 40 francs in cash and 300 in credit. Luckily, the boutique was a success and very popular among the city's social set.

When her daughter was born in 1897, Lanvin began making clothing for Marguerite. Her designs were so beautiful that her customers requested she make clothing for their children. Soon, sales for Lanvin's luxury children's wear surpassed her hat sales, and she decided to start designing matching outfits for mothers and daughters.

A businesswoman through and through, Lanvin knew the power of a good brand. She decided to embody her business

"Modern clothes need a certain romantic feel.'

– Jeanne Lanvin

with an image of mother and daughter, which makes me think of my own daughter whenever I see it. The iconic logo was actually inspired by a photo of Lanvin and her daughter dressed in matching costumes at a party, which was then illustrated by Paul Iribe (who was incidentally Coco Chanel's lover in the 1930s – when it comes to French fashion, everyone seems to be connected).

Lanvin's inquisitive nature saw her travel the world, a pursuit that widely influenced her approach to design. She famously kept a travel diary and collected fabric samples, embroidery, beads and whatever else she could take home to include in her inspiration library.

Utterly feminine and graceful, Lanvin's gowns were typically sleeveless and loose fitting with empire waistlines, influenced by the elegant looks of the eighteenth century. Women who wore Lanvin appeared statuesque and ethereal; the straight-line, slip-like garments were inspired by Lanvin's travels to Egypt and fascination with classical Roman and ancient Greek styles. Her signature silhouette – the *robe de style* – became a defining look of the 1920s, providing a contrast to the dominating flapper style of the era. She adorned her pieces with rich beading, embroidery, pearls and ribbons from her journeys. She would also embellish with romantic ruffles of fabric, which have continued to appear in Lanvin collections to this day. Fall 2013 Ready-to-Wear featured amazing skirts and tops created from nothing but ruffles.

Influenced by her exotic discoveries, Lanvin became experimental with her design methods and invested in her own dye factory so that she could produce fabrics in colours exclusive to her house. Most famously it was the signature Lanvin blue, inspired by the frescoes of Renaissance painter Fra Angelico, that would become synonymous with the label, but pinks, greens, red, black and metallic silver all became part of the label's DNA.

The mother–daughter narrative of Lanvin continued to motivate the company to reach new heights in the early decades of the new century. In 1927 Lanvin designed a perfume for her daughter's thirtieth birthday called Arpège, which even today is one of the world's most recognisable scents. Lanvin was one of the first fashion houses to expand into fragrance (after the classic Chanel No.5), and Lanvin continued to see new opportunities to create beautiful products – the same decade saw the launch of a stylish sports line selling swimming, tennis and riding wear and accessories. During the 1920s this smart businesswoman had twenty-three ateliers and almost 800 employees working for her fashion house.

Lanvin worked until her death in 1946, when her daughter, now known as Marie-Blanche, appropriately assumed control of the family business and became president. She worked as head designer until 1950, creating clothes that were reminiscent of her mother's ultra-feminine looks.

Following Marie-Blanche's departure, many creative directors have kept the Lanvin legacy alive but none more so than Alber Elbaz. Taking the reins from 2001 to 2015, he is credited with reviving the brand for twenty-first-century mothers and daughters.

I was so inspired by Elbaz and his fun, theatrical designs during his tenure at Lanvin. His take on French fashion is unique: unlike many other French labels who follow the path of simplicity, Elbaz's approach at Lanvin was excessive in the best possible way. He took the very best of Lanvin's original designs (the chemise silhouette, millinery and sparkly embellishments) and reinvented them in an avant-garde style that has since become legendary. When I think of Lanvin now, I am instantly reminded of the candy-store pink ruffle-sleeved dress from Elbaz's Spring 2010 Ready-to-Wear collection – it had a 1980s glamour to it but looked so very elegant on the runway.

Lanvin's outfits are so remarkable that when I was given the chance to own a miniature version, I did not think twice. I was halfway through one of my book tours in Europe and my luggage was already over capacity. I knew I definitely should not bring anything else home and had a 'look only' policy when shopping ... until I walked into Lanvin's flagship store in Paris. There in front of me was a limited-edition Lanvin doll wearing a long black tulle skirt with a chic black blazer, bow tie and smart hat, holding a red balloon. Worst of all, she was the last one available for purchase. She was magnificent. Even though I had to carry her on my lap on every plane ride for the rest of the book tour, I did not regret buying her. She now sits in my studio in pride of place and I get to enjoy a little bit of Lanvin every day.

Jeanne Lanvin was a woman ahead of her time: a mother and an entrepreneur who melded the two to start a fashion empire with heart. Lanvin designs continue to celebrate the power and romance of femininity, and they will be worn by mothers and daughters for decades to come.

LANVIN
PARIS

LANVIN
PARIS

Fall
2013

Ready-to-
Wear

LANVIN
PARIS

Fall
2012

Ready-to-
Wear

LANVIN
PARIS

Fall
2010

Ready-to-
Wear

05

Givenchy

GIVENCHY
PARIS

The essence of Givenchy is a designer and his muse. I am of course referring to one of the most famous partnerships in fashion history, between designer Hubert de Givenchy and actress Audrey Hepburn. The pair met fortuitously in France in 1953 and the rest was history. Their first encounter sparked an enduring friendship that would last decades. That friendship inspired the look and feel of the Givenchy style.

Givenchy was born into an aristocratic family in Beauvais, northern France, in 1927. Tragedy struck when Givenchy's father died unexpectedly, leaving three-year-old Hubert to be raised by his mother and paternal grandparents. Givenchy's grandfather was an avid traveller and collected fabrics and exotic ephemera when he was abroad. He observed his young grandson's fascination with his souvenirs, and would allow him to play with them if he did well in school. As a result Givenchy became a star pupil.

Givenchy's burgeoning interest in fashion and design was also fostered by his mother and grandmother, and as a child he was enthralled by the work of Spanish designer Cristóbal Balenciaga. At age ten, Givenchy attempted to leave home on a quest to personally deliver some of his illustrations to his idol. Unsurprisingly, he didn't get far; his mother found him and took him home, but it showed his determined spirit and early interest in fashion.

At age seventeen, Givenchy left home again – and this time for good, when he enrolled in the École des Beaux-Arts in Paris. While studying he worked as an apprentice for French fashion designer Jacques Fath, and upon graduating he began moving

'Luxury is in each detail.'

– Hubert de Givenchy

between some of the most revered couturiers of the time: Robert Piguet, Lucien Lelong and Elsa Schiaparelli, in turn. Givenchy's experience amassed quickly and his reputation as a sought-after designer spread throughout Paris.

In 1952 Givenchy started his namesake house, and it didn't take long for him to become as respected as his previous mentors. In fact, his success was instant: the first look to hit the runway, a white ruffle-sleeved blouse worn by Italian actress Bettina Graziani, became one of his most iconic designs. The blouse, quickly dubbed the 'Bettina blouse', was part of Givenchy's collection of separates, comprising tops and bottoms that could be mixed and matched. While it is difficult to imagine clothing without separates now, this was a revolutionary concept at the time because it gave women greater wardrobe choice: they could pick what suited them and dress for comfort and individual style. Givenchy's flexible designs captivated women across the globe and became staple items in every fashion lover's wardrobe.

It was during this first year of Givenchy's new fashion house that Audrey Hepburn found her way to his atelier. She had been sent by the production team of the film *Sabrina*, in which she starred, to buy some French clothing she could wear on screen. Legend has it that Givenchy was expecting Katharine Hepburn and was surprised to meet the other Hepburn in a pair of capri pants and a Venetian gondolier's wide-brim hat. Her intuitive style was undeniable. Givenchy's muse had arrived.

Givenchy and Hepburn would go on to collaborate for the next forty years, until Hepburn's death in 1993. Givenchy designed collections with Hepburn at the forefront. He created modern and chic clothes that women like her – or women who aspired to be like her – enjoyed wearing, including everything from evening gowns to casual capri pants with oversized white men's shirts. He supplied wardrobe for Hepburn's films *Funny Face, Paris When It Sizzles* and, most famously, *Breakfast at Tiffany's*, in which Holly Golightly's long black dress, pearl necklace and satin gloves became a worldwide sensation. Audrey Hepburn was also the face of the Givenchy perfume L'Interdit.

Throughout the 1950s and 1960s Givenchy embraced youth culture. In 1954 he invented the shirt-dress silhouette that is still worn today. The shape later evolved into the sack dress, which he co-designed with none other than Balenciaga. Givenchy's childhood dream of meeting his fashion idol had finally been realised in 1953. Even better, the Spanish designer took an interest in Givenchy and became his personal friend and mentor. Givenchy was inspired by Balenciaga's architectural, structured clothing and straight lines, which would inform the design DNA of his own fashion house.

Givenchy worked up until his retirement in 1995. He created a fashion empire that spoke to generations of women who yearned for refined simplicity and paved the way for his successors John Galliano, Alexander McQueen, Julien Macdonald, Riccardo Tisci and Clare Waight Keller to continue his work with poise and sophistication.

Tisci had a very strong impact in his twelve years at the house and was particularly celebrated for his couture designs. He became known for dramatic gowns in simple black or white

> 'To have style is
> to have feeling for
> what is currently
> fashionable and still to
> simultaneously remain
> true to oneself.'
>
> – Hubert de Givenchy

but with fantastically intricate embellishments. The incredible beading and feathered designs in the Fall 2010 and 2011 Couture collections are perfect examples of this. These 'modern fairytale' looks won him many celebrity fans who wanted to make a statement on the red carpet, continuing the theme of dressing some of the world's most high-profile women.

Waight Keller, who has been at the helm since only 2017, has already contributed to the Givenchy legacy by designing a dress for a true modern fairytale: Meghan Markle's marriage to Prince Harry. It's no secret that I love a royal wedding. I was so in awe of how stunning Meghan Markle looked as she walked down the aisle in Givenchy that I felt compelled to capture the moment. I illustrated the new princess in her dress for my own Instagram and within moments it was being shared everywhere and became my most reposted illustration on social media.

True inspiration can lead to the greatest of all creations and this was the case when Givenchy found his muse in Audrey Hepburn. Their enduring forty-year friendship allowed Givenchy to design with empathy – understanding that he was no longer designing for women but for the woman. I kept that in mind a few years ago when I was lucky to be given the opportunity to illustrate the modern-day Givenchy woman for their fragrance Live Irrésistible. Each woman has her own story, and Givenchy provides a way to tell it through fashion.

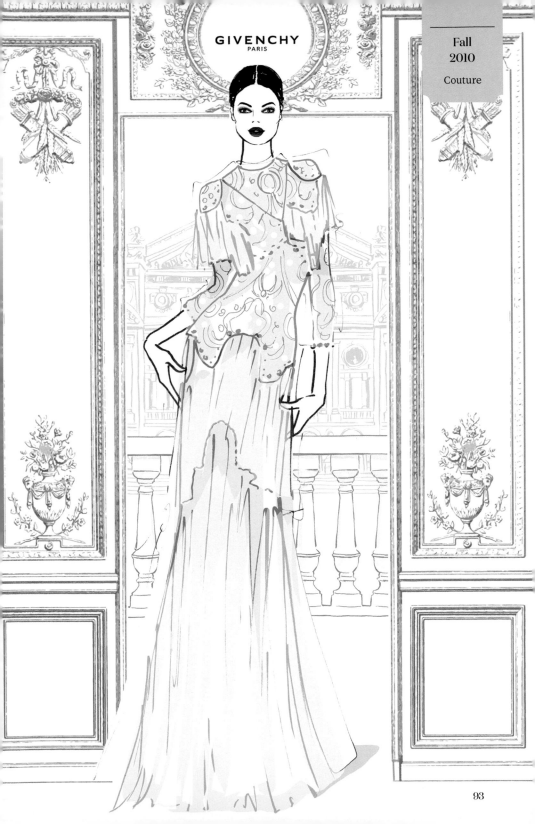

GIVENCHY
PARIS

GIVENCHY
PARIS

GIVENCHY
PARIS

Spring
2016

Ready-to-
Wear

06

Chloé

I f you're looking for an haute couture label that truly
understands women, then look no further than Chloé.
Since its inception in 1952 by founder Gaby Aghion, it's been
the house for women's fashion designed almost exclusively
by women.

The rich history of its pioneering women starts with
Aghion and her life far from France. Aghion was born
Gabrielle Hanoka in 1921 in Alexandria, Egypt. Her father
owned a tobacco factory and she lived a comfortable life,
receiving a French education and going on to study political
science at university. Aghion's introduction to fashion came
via her mother, who was besotted with French fashion and
often had custom pieces designed by Egyptian seamstresses,
inspired by the spreads she saw in French magazines.

The lure of Paris was always on the horizon for Aghion. She
moved to the city with her childhood sweetheart and husband,
Raymond Aghion, just after World War II. The pair quickly
immersed themselves in the liberal arts and cafe society of their
new home, befriending the likes of Pablo Picasso and writers
including Louis Aragon and Lawrence Durrell. Café de Flore,
in the heart of the Left Bank, became the Aghions' local haunt,
the centre of a burgeoning intellectual and creative scene.
Aghion's introduction to this new world sparked an insatiable
desire to do something for herself instead of depending on her
husband financially. She craved independence.

Aghion saw an opportunity to make clothing for women who
were young and free in spirit, regardless of age – women who
did not comply with the status quo. And thus in 1952 she started
a fashion house, with business partner Jacques Lenoir coming

'All I've ever wanted
was for Chloé to have
a happy spirit, to make
people happy.'

– Gaby Aghion

on board in 1953. Many of her friends thought the project was simply a manifestation of Aghion's boredom and would not last. Driven and ambitious, Aghion proved them all wrong.

While many of her fashion contemporaries named their labels after themselves, Aghion's family forbade her to do so. They could not understand why she wanted or needed to work, given the family's wealth. They believed the reputation of the Aghion name would be tainted if it were used commercially. Aghion instead borrowed the name of a friend, Chloé Huysmans, who personified the essence of the label that she wanted to create.

Aghion launched her first collection at Café de Flore over breakfast. Today designers are always looking for innovative ways to launch collections, and it's not unheard of to attend fashion shows in garages, swimming pools and cafes. But at the time, serving fashion with croissants was unheard of; most collections were simply previewed in private ateliers. That kind of boldness is at the heart of Chloé's cool-girl chic.

Chloé's first collection consisted of six poplin dresses, which Aghion designed before sourcing the fabric and then hiring an haute couture seamstress to bring them to life. The dresses were inspired by luxury sportswear that she had observed women wearing in Egypt but that had yet to cross the waters to Paris. The dresses evoked femininity in soft pastels, with a tennis-court-meets-cocktail-bar aesthetic, and soon became a wardrobe staple among Aghion's bohemian clique.

Aghion's alternative approach to fashion was in direct opposition to the opulence of haute couture culture in the height of Dior's New Look era. Aghion distinguished herself with her signature carefree and stripped-back elegance, and was the pioneer of informal formal wear.

She was also innovative in her business decisions. Chloé was one of the first houses to remove the wait times and fittings of haute couture and offer *prêt-à-porter* clothing. Aghion believed fashion should be accessible to all, and allowing customers to buy clothes off the rack immediately was one way of achieving this. She originally took to the streets, selling her dresses out of a suitcase to boutiques until she sold out. She challenged the status quo yet again by keeping the Chloé label on each piece (at the time, it was customary for boutiques to use their own labels for ready-to-wear clothing). In many ways, Chloé changed the way we dress and shop forever.

Given her history of making bold business decisions, it was little surprise that Aghion decided to step down from the brand at the height of her career to foster emerging talent. She hired fresh young designers including Gérard Pipart, Maxime de la Falaise, Michèle Rosier, Graziella Fontana and, perhaps her most famous discovery, Karl Lagerfeld, who worked on and off at the house as creative director for close to thirty years and helped secure its position as the go-to label for ultra-feminine bohemian chic looks. Chloé continues to be known as the launch pad for the illustrious careers of many designers.

From the 1990s onwards (aside from a brief stint by Paulo Melim Andersson), Chloé has been a house led by a league of extraordinary women. In 1997 Stella McCartney, aged twenty-five and fresh out of Central Saint Martins college, took the lead at Chloé, giving the label a little rock-and-roll flair. Following McCartney was her Saint Martins classmate

> ## 'Fashion should be as fresh as a salad.'
>
> – Gaby Aghion

Phoebe Philo, who was responsible for the 'it' bag of the 2000s: the Paddington. Sequential posts by Hannah MacGibbon, Clare Waight Keller and present creative director Natacha Ramsay-Levi have all maintained Chloé's unique aesthetic.

MacGibbon was only with the brand for three years, but in that time she created some of my favourite Chloé looks that feel both wearable and impossibly beautiful. Chloé to me is the dreamy French girl that I imagine skipping through the Jardin des Tuileries in central Paris wearing the ethereal white pleated tiered maxi dress from MacGibbon's Spring 2010 Ready-to-Wear collection.

When I'm sipping my café au lait at Café de Flore I always think of the original Chloé show there. The cafe is one of my favourite places to visit in Paris – not only are the pastries excellent but it's steeped in fashion history. I love how the house of Chloé has always followed its own path and made its own rules, in line with its founder and original cool girl, Gaby Aghion. Chloé gives free-spirited women the confidence to be themselves ... and might just inspire them to skip around the Tuileries as well.

Chloé

Chloé

Chloé

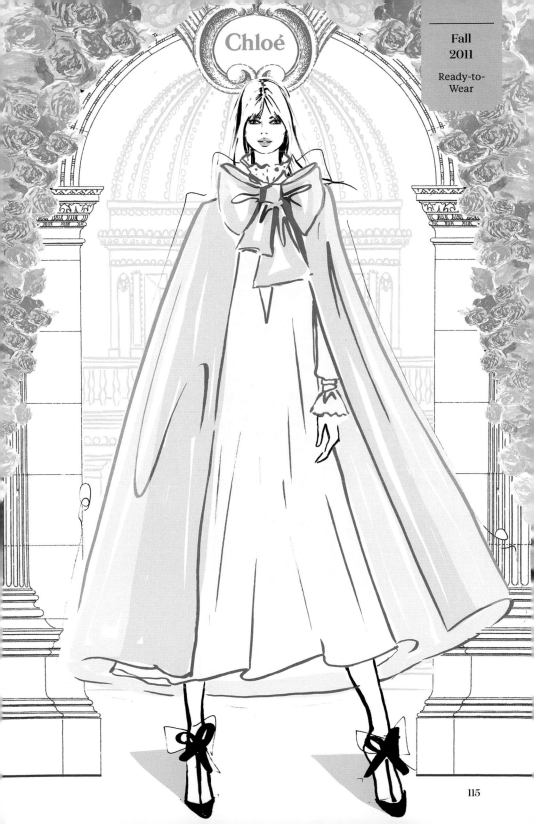

Chloé

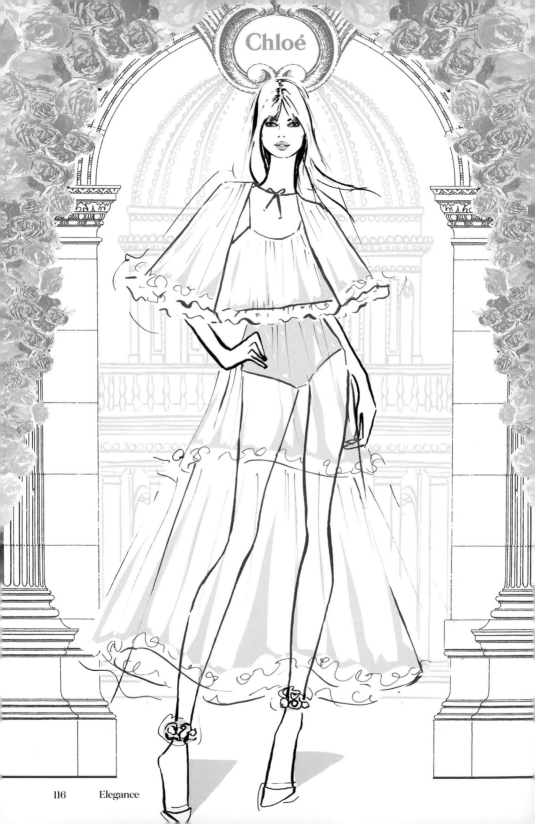

07

Balmain

In our internet culture Balmain is the fashion house that receives the most likes, but the brand isn't just a trend – it's timeless. The label's history spans seventy years from the post–World War II era to today's #BalmainArmy. At the core of this longevity is Pierre Balmain, the man who started it all. His fastidious attention to detail and fashion sketches are worthy of the most prestigious gallery walls.

Pierre Balmain's start in life was similar to that of some of his fellow French fashion contemporaries: he came from a wealthy family who unexpectedly found themselves with next to nothing. Born in 1914, Pierre Balmain was only seven when his father, who owned a drapery business, died. Tragedy often spawns opportunity, and his father's death was young Balmain's forced entry into the world of fashion. Balmain and his sister had always played in their mother's fashion boutique making paper dolls; now they had to work there.

In 1933, upon leaving school, Balmain attended the École des Beaux-Arts, where he studied architecture. However, it wasn't long before he moved back into fashion, working part-time as a freelance illustrator for Robert Piguet. A year into his studies, he left art school and Piguet behind when he was offered a job with Paris-based British designer Edward Molyneux. In the five years that Balmain worked for Molyneux, he learned the skills required to be a first-class couturier, skills that would guide him through the rest of his professional career.

In a similar narrative to many of his fashion contemporaries – including Christian Dior and Yves Saint Laurent – Balmain left his post at Molyneux when he was called up for compulsory military service. After his army duties

'Keep to the basic principles of fashion and you will always be in harmony with the latest trends without falling prey to them.'

– Pierre Balmain

he began a new role at Lucien Lelong, where he met fellow emerging designer Dior, also recently discharged.

Balmain and Dior quickly became friends, so much so that Balmain actually invited Dior to go into partnership with him and start a label together. When Dior declined, Balmain went solo, opening his namesake house in 1945. A healthy rivalry developed between the two designers, who both championed the hourglass silhouette and cinched-waist with bouffant skirt look that excited women after the fashion restrictions of World War II.

While Dior was credited as the father of the New Look, Balmain met similar success with a distinctive look of his own. Balmain's first collection featured lavish strapless evening gowns in greens, browns and lavenders – shades that were fresh to the runway and women's wardrobes – along with long bell-shaped skirts and two-piece suits that could transition from day to night. His designs were uncomplicated, with straight lines and simple shapes that were applauded by the press. In fact, Balmain's close friend Gertrude Stein reviewed the show for *Vogue* and described him as the young designer to watch. Balmain quickly amassed a string of loyal celebrity clients, including actresses Marlene Dietrich, Katharine Hepburn and Vivien Leigh, and was even dubbed 'the king of French fashion'.

One of his admirers in this period was Danish designer Erik Mortensen, who became Balmain's assistant and later his partner in life and business.

When Balmain died in 1982, Mortensen became his successor. Mortensen designed seventeen collections during his time at Balmain as head designer. He was followed by Hervé Pierre, who took over for two years in 1990.

One of the Balmain brand's most successful periods came between 1992 and 2002 when Oscar de la Renta took the helm as creative director. De la Renta already had decades of experience as a successful designer behind him when he started at Balmain, and he restored the old-school elegance that was the signature of the house's founder. Red carpet looks on adoring celebrities put Balmain on the international stage once again.

Most recently, the name on everyone's lips is Olivier Rousteing. Another fashion wunderkind, Rousteing was only twenty-five when he received the top job at Balmain, joining the label as creative director in 2011. His astute flair for style and refreshingly youthful approach to fashion has seen him garner a younger audience for one of France's oldest fashion houses.

Rousteing has cemented the label's strong look of structured and embellished decadence. He effortlessly brings together opposing forces with a mix of sharp, tailored, almost tough military-like silhouettes and delicate details, including fine beading and studded work. I love his sense of baroque style – no one else can compile a look of thigh-high slouch boots and a long-sleeved mini dress with Balmain's signature gold detailing (Fall 2016 Ready-to-Wear) or pair a black and silver jacquard print with a laser-cut silk floor-length dress (Spring 2013 Ready-to-Wear). Rousteing dares to be different and it always pays off.

> **'Good fashion is evolution, not revolution.'**
>
> – Pierre Balmain

Rousteing has also been applauded for bringing diversity to French haute couture and making fashion inclusive to all, from his campaigns to the runway. Rousteing embodies the next generation of French fashion with his open-mindedness, risk-taking sensibility and understanding of what it means to be a designer in the new millennium. He was one of the first to embrace Instagram, and Balmain's social media clout is now the highest of any haute couture label.

I'm a proud member of the #BalmainArmy, and I'm reminded of it every day when I work at my desk, beneath a framed Balmain commission. I was asked to create something special with one of my characters for Balmain's fragrance Extatic. Balmain's French headquarters loved it so much that they also requested a framed version to hang in *their* offices, and you can imagine how ecstatic I was! It's one of my proudest career moments – I love that we share the same artwork in our offices on opposite sides of the world.

Balmain's creations are not for wallflowers – they are bold, outlandish statement pieces designed to exude confidence. I am excited to see where Rousteing takes the next generation of French haute couture.

Fall
2016

Ready-to-
Wear

BALMAIN
PARIS

Fall
2012

Ready-to-
Wear

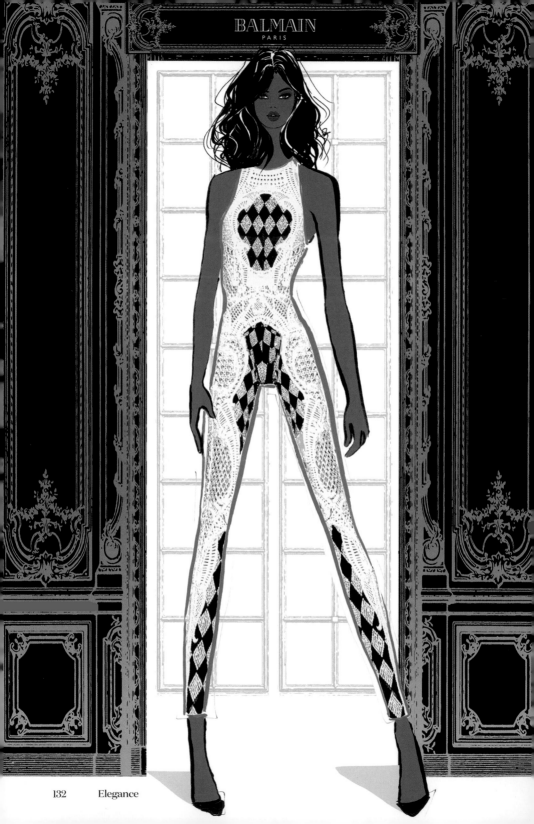

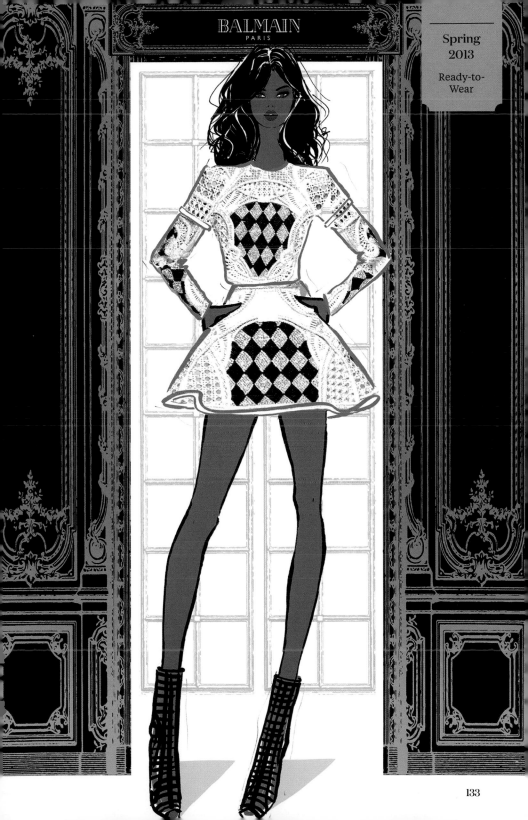

BALMAIN
PARIS

Spring
2013

Ready-to-
Wear

BALMAIN

PARIS

Spring
2016

Ready-to-
Wear

08

Louis Vuitton

Believe it or not, luggage as we know it today is the creation of mastermind Louis Vuitton. For Vuitton, luggage was not just a portable storage device but the protector of beloved possessions, and therefore it deserved to be treated with respect. This ethos is still embraced by the label today. What started as a modest travel goods business almost 170 years ago, designed to get customers to their destination in style, has evolved into a fashion empire where style is the destination.

Appropriately, Louis Vuitton travelled many steps before opening his eponymous label in 1854, quite literally. After his mother died when he was a young boy, Vuitton's father remarried a woman who treated her new stepson with contempt. Dreaming of another life, at age thirteen Vuitton decided to leave his home in Anchay for Paris – on foot. This ambitious journey was 470 kilometres long and took two years to complete, with Vuitton taking odd jobs to secure food and shelter along the way.

Finally arriving in Paris, Vuitton was ready to start a life for himself and found a job as an apprentice with Romain Maréchal, a box maker and packer. Members of a respected profession in the early nineteenth century, box makers and packers personally designed and packed durable luggage for society's elite before they embarked on travel by train, horse and carriage or boat. Working closely with Maréchal, Vuitton learned his new craft firsthand from one of the city's most revered luggage specialists, and quickly developed a name for himself as a key talent in the industry.

After seventeen years working for Maréchal, Vuitton finally opened his own business on rue Neuve-des-Capucines in 1854. Recently married, the thirty-three-year-old believed his

'The Louis Vuitton woman is more about a quality – a quality within some women that needs to come forward, to be noticed and recognised.'

– Marc Jacobs

own shop would offer a greater opportunity to provide for his growing family. He was right.

Vuitton put the customer first by creating products that were equally stylish and functional, and he struck gold when he invented the first flat-topped trunk. Far more stackable and travel friendly than its curved predecessors, the new trunk was a sensation.

Vuitton's design innovations continued to add to his success. He exchanged leather for his patented grey Trianon canvas, making his bags more lightweight, and developed fabrics that were both durable and waterproof. Vuitton's designs even attracted the attention of the most important woman in France at the time, Napoleon III's wife, the Empress Eugénie, who employed the designer to be her personal box maker and packer. Her patronage led to a surge in popularity and Vuitton was able to expand his business. In 1859 he opened his famous Asnières atelier (which is still in operation today) to keep up with demand.

As Louis Vuitton's popularity rose, the ageing designer enlisted his son, Georges Vuitton, to work in the business and eventually become his successor, which Georges did after his father's death in 1892. Georges Vuitton was also a visionary and entrepreneur in equal measure. In 1896 when his father's original designs were subject to counterfeit reproductions, he designed the famous LV monogrammed pattern with quatrefoil and flowers because copying a monogram at the time was illegal. Georges Vuitton also invented the first unpickable lock, a breakthrough design used to protect the contents of suitcases stowed away on travels.

By 1913, Louis Vuitton was the largest travel goods brand in the world and had opened a store on the famous Champs-Élysées strip in Paris.

Working up until his death in 1936, Georges Vuitton passed on the company reins to his son Gaston-Louis Vuitton, marking the third generation of Vuitton men running the company.

Gaston-Louis Vuitton introduced leather accessories into the Louis Vuitton family with the Papillon bag, an elegant cylindrical shoulder bag that made its debut in 1966. Slowly the house was moving towards a larger fashion offering but Louis Vuitton's first ready-to-wear collection was still a long way off – about thirty years, in fact.

Taking a leather-goods label to the runway is no easy feat, but Marc Jacobs did it effortlessly. Appointed creative director in 1997, Jacobs led the brand from iconic luggage to coveted wardrobe must-haves, taking inspiration from the company's travel heritage. He designed luxurious pieces that could be stowed away in your Louis Vuitton bag and taken on vacation: the look was fun and stylish, whimsical and edgy.

One of my favourite Louis Vuitton fashion looks was Jacobs' playful homage to Louis Vuitton's signature monogram print when he designed a cropped vinyl jacket bearing the logo for his Fall 2003 Ready-to-Wear collection. This retro look – complete with leather driving gloves – feels like the ultimate travel outfit. Or perhaps that honour goes to the three-piece caramel coat set from the Fall 2012 Ready-to-Wear collection. For this show, models were appropriately accompanied down the runway by luggage porters in gold-trimmed caps, carrying the stylish leather handbags and carryalls that matched each jetsetting look.

'Fashion is there
to break any frontier
possible.'

– Nicolas Ghesquière

Following Jacobs' departure in 2014, Nicolas Ghesquière held creative sway at Louis Vuitton until 2018, when he began sharing the honour with Virgil Abloh. While Ghesquière remained head of womenswear, Abloh took the creative lead for menswear, and his debut collection became the fastest-selling range in Louis Vuitton's history.

For me, Louis Vuitton has always been about the spirit of travel. I travel a lot for work and having such a beautifully crafted object in which to store my things makes me feel a little closer to home. It's the fashion house for people on the go, and the works I have illustrated for the label always come back to this sentiment. It was the inspiration behind an animation I designed to coincide with a range of new Louis Vuitton sneakers, in which one of my characters travelled through New York on a Louis Vuitton skateboard wearing her new shoes.

Quality and fine craftsmanship have seen Louis Vuitton prosper through almost two centuries. Longevity like this is rare and just goes to show that when you build a product to last, so will the brand.

LOUIS VUITTON

LOUIS VUITTON

09

Hermès

Not many families can say they've worked together for six generations. At 180 years and counting, Hermès is one of the oldest family-operated businesses in France. Hermès is also one of my favourite French labels. They are connoisseurs of extreme elegance with their beautiful screen-printed *carrés* (silk scarves) and covetable hand-stitched Birkin bags.

You only need to look as far as Hermès' famous horse and carriage logo to see the origin of the label. The Hermès dynasty began with Thierry Hermès, who in 1837 opened a harness workshop in the Grands Boulevards district of Paris. Here he made horse harnesses and bridles, and quickly developed a loyal following among the bourgeoisie. In 1855, he received a first-class medal in the Paris Exposition for his work. Passing away in 1878, he left his son, Charles-Émile, to take over the business.

Charles-Émile expanded the label's offering and introduced leather accessories and saddlery. This included the first Hermès bag, designed to allow riders to carry their gear with them. Retiring in 1902, he passed on the baton to his sons, Émile-Maurice and Adolphe. The pair worked together for nearly two decades, but in 1920 Émile-Maurice became the sole custodian.

Émile-Maurice oversaw Hermès' most defining period as he shifted the business from horseriding accessories to luxury fashion. He introduced the label's first haute couture women's line and the iconic silk scarves, and even designed the first Hermès handbag – inspired by his father's original saddlery bag – for his wife.

Like his grandfather and father, Émile-Maurice was a true businessman. While travelling in North America in 1916, he

'The main strength of Hermès is the love of craftsmanship.'

– Axel Dumas in *Forbes*

met Henry Ford and saw the Ford factories in operation. Not only was Émile-Maurice inspired to expand his own business, but he also made one of his greatest discoveries: the zip. After seeing zippers being used for the roofs of cars, he sought the exclusive European rights to the new fastener for two years. Émile-Maurice was going to use the zip in fashion for the first time, to fasten Hermès saddlery bags.

Soon the zip was being referred to as the 'Hermès fastener' all over Europe. It became so popular that the Duke of Windsor requested a golf jacket with a zip fastening designed by Hermès, and Coco Chanel even visited the Hermès atelier to learn how the zip functioned.

Jean-Louis Dumas, the grandson of Émile-Maurice Hermès, toook the reins in 1978 and also left an influential legacy. After a chance encounter on a plane between Jean-Louis and actress Jane Birkin, the two collaborated to create one of the world's most coveted accessories: the Birkin bag. Each Birkin is still handmade in France and can take up to twenty-five hours to complete. The waitlist to procure such an iconic piece extends to five years. A Birkin bag has been known to be a more worthwhile investment than stocks or gold.

It was during Émile-Maurice Hermès' time at the head of the brand that it gained one of its most iconic symbols: Hermès Orange. Originally the colour choice was just a matter of necessity: after World War II, there was a shortage of the cream boxes that the brand had been using, so Hermès had to go with whatever was left. The distinctive orange packaging is now synonymous with luxury fashion and a clear signifier of the beautiful object within.

Hermès have a knack for designing accessories that take on a life of their own. In a similar category to the Birkin is the Kelly bag. Originally designed in 1930, the bag became famous when a photograph appeared in *Life* magazine of the actress Grace Kelly using the handbag to conceal her pregnant belly.

Another design that's stood the test of time is the Hermès silk scarf, which originally debuted in 1937, made from raw Chinese silk spun into yarn. Grace Kelly was also a famous collector of the scarves, along with Audrey Hepburn and Jackie Onassis. Today, reportedly, an Hermès silk scarf is sold somewhere in the world every twenty seconds and the brand has produced thousands of stunning designs.

While I do not buy an Hermès silk scarf every twenty seconds, I have become an avid collector. One of my most treasured possessions is an Hermès scarf that was given to me for Mother's Day when my daughter was four years old. She knew I loved collecting the special silk scarves in my closet and asked her father to buy one for me. My husband was unable to resist her sweet notion and took her to Hermès' Collins Street store in Melbourne, where she proceeded to get up on the counter and sift through all the scarves – unaware that she was in a very nice shop! The amazing Hermès staff indulged her and she ended up choosing a scarf all by herself. The design she chose is incredible; I wear it all the time with pride.

Hermès' refined yet opulent looks really attracted international attention in the late 1990s and onwards when Martin Margiela, Jean Paul Gaultier and Christophe Lemaire all had posts as creative directors.

> '**I wouldn't go anywhere important without my own favourite Hermès black bag ... For me, going out without that purse would seem almost like going out naked. Well, almost.**'
>
> – Grace Kelly

The Hermès style to me is embodied in riding pants and boots with tailored blazers, and of course silk scarves and one of their iconic leather handbags– *à la* one of my favourite collections by Gaultier, Spring 2008 Ready-to-Wear. For Gaultier's Spring 2011 Ready-to-Wear collection, runway models accessorised their jodhpurs with riding crops and miniature saddle bags. I love that the spirit of the stables still lives on at Hermès today, nearly two centuries since the house's origin.

The house is now led by Nadège Vanhee-Cybulski and continues to produce fashion looks inspired by Hermès' equestrian heritage, as seen in her Fall 2017 Ready-to-Wear Range, which featured blue leather riding pants and retro colours spanning silk garments. Why wear a scarf when you could have a whole Hermès silk dress?

In a world of fast fashion it is comforting to know that brands such as Hermès still exist. Hermès never expedites their output to chase a trend. Instead they take their time and continue to make most of their bags by hand in France – it's a slow process but worth the wait for the end result. I know when I buy a piece from an Hermès collection, it's not just a scarf or a bag – it's a future heirloom, and if I'm lucky it might also last six generations.

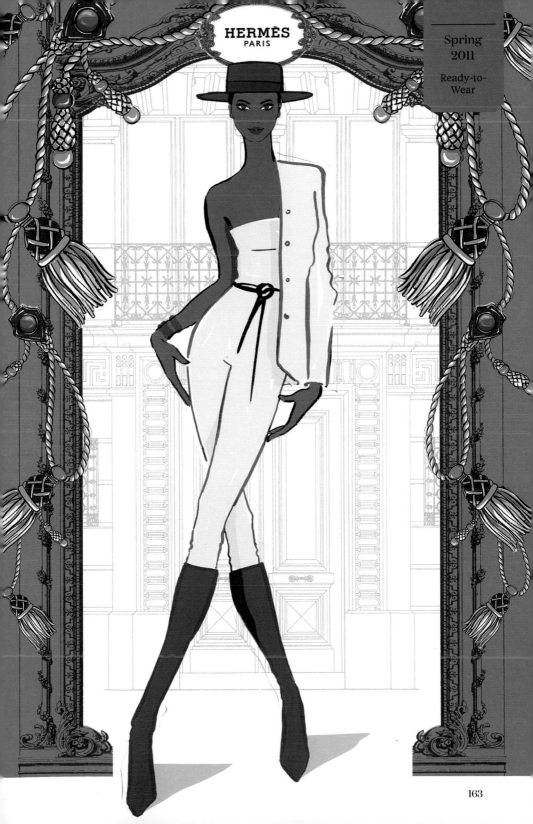

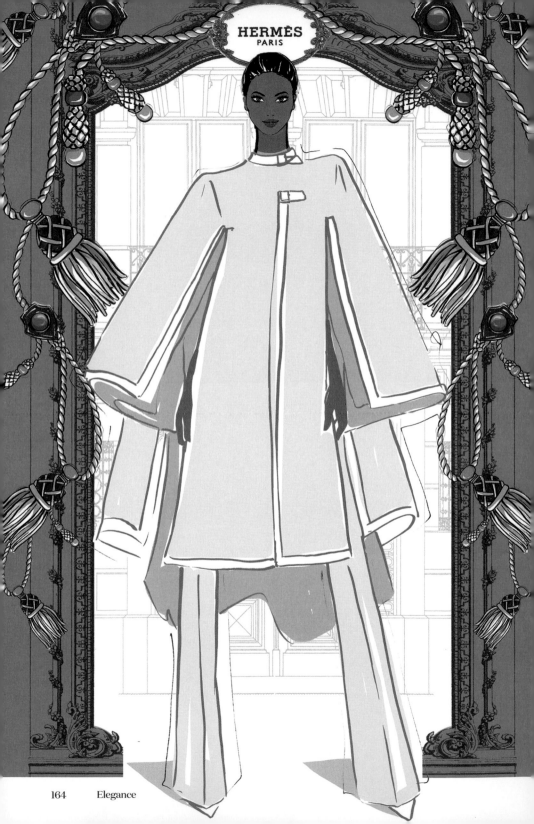

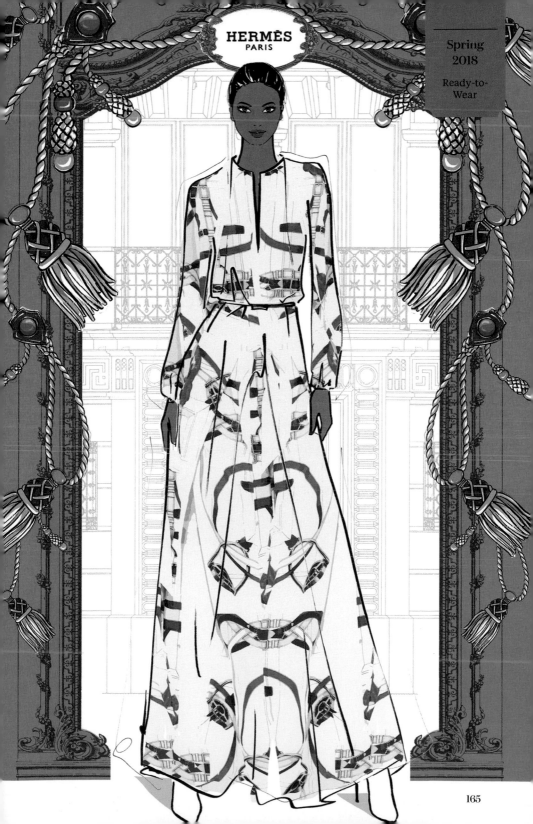

HERMÈS
PARIS

Spring
2018

Ready-to-
Wear

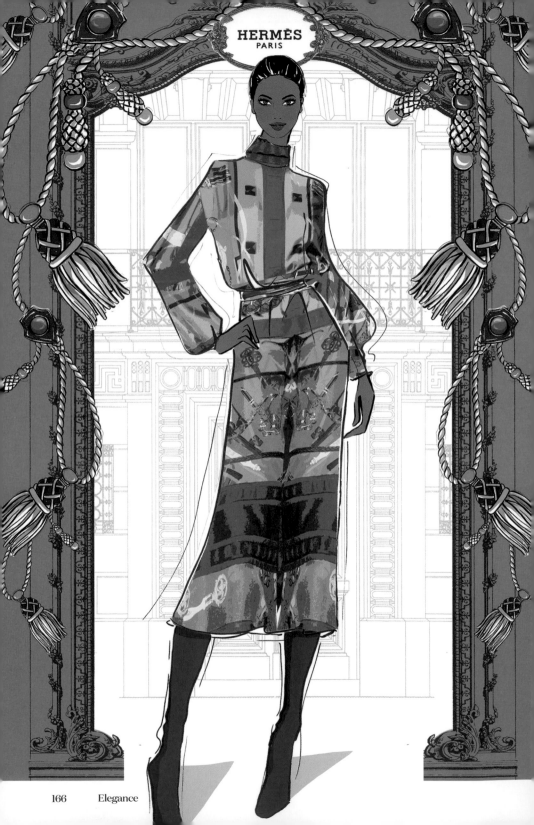

HERMÈS
PARIS

HERMÈS
PARIS

Fall
2017

Ready-to-
Wear

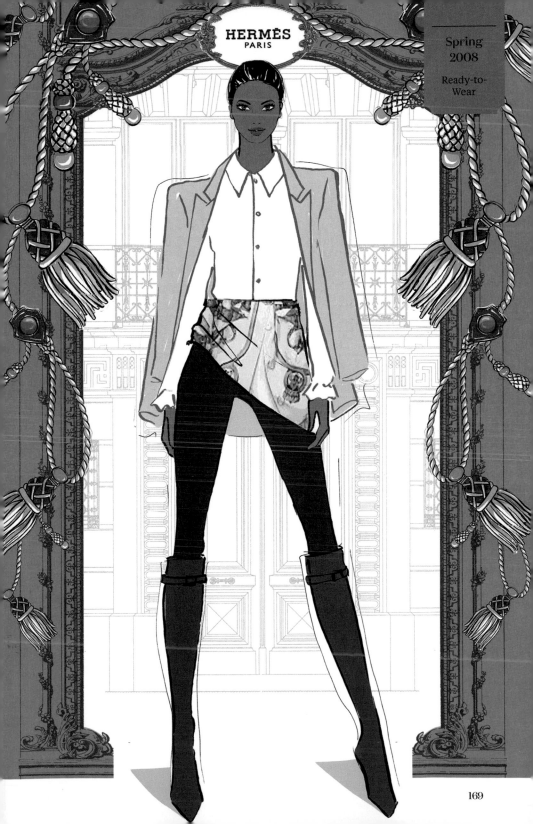

HERMÈS
PARIS

Spring
2008

Ready-to-
Wear

10

Celine

French fashion is popularly associated with couture culture, and rightly so, with its intricate, layered and detailed looks that are worthy of every accolade. Celine is different: the label has approached the same design applications with a minimalist touch, making their collections accessible for the everyday. I think one of the secrets of the intrinsic French style emanates from Celine; they have set the tone for the modern French woman's day-to-day wardrobe, and are internationally recognised as the pioneers of chic simplicity.

This minimalist philosophy stems from Celine's founder, Céline Vipiana. Vipiana started her business in 1945 with her husband, Richard, but it was a long way from the womenswear we recognise Celine for today. Instead, the couple designed and sold made-to-measure children's footwear. Their first boutique at 52 rue de Malte in Paris quickly grew a loyal clientele, and by 1958 the Vipiana duo had opened three additional boutiques.

It took until 1960 for Vipiana to change design direction and introduce womenswear to her repertoire. The world was entering a time of liberation and fashion followed suit. Hems were shortened and silhouettes loosened – women resisted the tightly cinched waistlines of the 1950s New Look and wanted clothing that was comfortable, stylish and ultimately for them. Vipiana understood this and started designing clothing that reflected this new era.

Vipiana's vision was to design and curate collections that celebrated modern minimalism. She favoured the idea of women investing in quality items that could be worn season after season instead of chasing trend-based fashion and

'Build a wardrobe rather than focusing on trends.'

– Phoebe Philo

growing tired of it as soon as it was hung in the wardrobe. She also favoured wardrobe staples over pieces reserved for rare special occasions. In a tight neutral palette of beige, tan, cream and grey – a palette that is still evidently so Celine fifty years later – Vipiana designed luxury sportswear paired with leather gloves, loafers and handbags that women could wear every day.

Celine became famous for designing practical clothing that did not skimp on style. Many of the original styles are still referenced and reinterpreted today, including Vipiana's wool skirt suits, leather vests, pastel-coloured denim and the original trench coat, which debuted in Celine's 1964 'American Sulky' collection.

Working as head designer until her passing in 1997, Vipiana continues to influence French fashion. Her legacy has remained so dominant due to the work of her design successors, most notably Michael Kors and Phoebe Philo. During her post at the creative helm of Celine from 2008 until 2018, Philo became the godmother of modern women's fashion. She understood Vipiana's minimalist style and embraced it to create the elite French chic wardrobe. Celine beams with her effortlessly cool style.

Similarly to Vipiana, Philo committed to a neutral colour palette of white, beige, pastels, caramels and black, using these colours to guide her sharp and interesting tailoring. It is as if the fabric is being folded origami-like into life. One of my favourite Philo looks emerged from her Spring 2018 Ready-to-Wear collection – the model on the runway wears a breezy quasi-trench coat layered over a full-body jumpsuit. It's the simplest of looks but could be worn all day, from running out to buy your morning baguette, to dinner at a fine-dining restaurant. It's the basic uniform of the French cool girl – and it makes you instantly want to pull it off yourself.

Following the lead of Vipiana, Philo also helped position Celine as the go-to label for quality basics. Investing in a handful of wardrobe staples, and wearing them interchangeably with equally good accessories and footwear, has become Celine's style mantra. Philo, alongside her leather and accessories director Johnny Coca (who worked at the label from 2010 to 2015), introduced a series of cult 'it' bags, including the Trapeze, the Luggage, the Trio and the Cabas, elevating Celine to the status of heritage brands such as Louis Vuitton and Hermès when it comes to leather goods.

Not forgetting Celine's early beginnings designing children's footwear, Philo kept the soul of the label very much alive when she designed the now famous glove shoe in the Spring 2015 Ready-to-Wear collection. I especially love how Philo styled the glove shoe with every runway look as part of this collection. These looks included another jumpsuit, this one in minimal white with a line of black buttons running right up one trouser leg and across the body. A jumpsuit feels like the perfect 'ready to wear' outfit for the modern woman – it's all about style, ease and comfort.

Philo's contributions to Celine also extend to the choices she made off the runway. Spring 2015 was one of Celine's most iconic campaigns, and not only because of the glove shoe. Philo cast then eighty-year-old acclaimed American writer

> '**Women should have choices, and women should feel good in what they wear.**'
>
> – Phoebe Philo

Joan Didion as the face of the campaign, making headlines around the world. Didion looked as chic as ever in oversized Celine sunglasses with her trademark bob hairstyle.

Hedi Slimane took over in 2018 and really made his mark – as he had done at Saint Laurent – by changing the brand name, in this case dropping the accent on the 'e' in 'Céline'.

A trip to Paris is incomplete without visiting Celine's avenue Montaigne flagship boutique. I believe it's here that you are able to witness the French fashion forecast before your very eyes. The pragmatic and almost utilitarian aesthetic of Celine is the epitome of simple dressing. It's fuss-free but deeply stylish in the subtlest way, allowing the woman who wears Celine to feel empowered. It's a way of dressing that is as alive today as it was in the 1960s – timeless, ageless and elegant.

CELINE

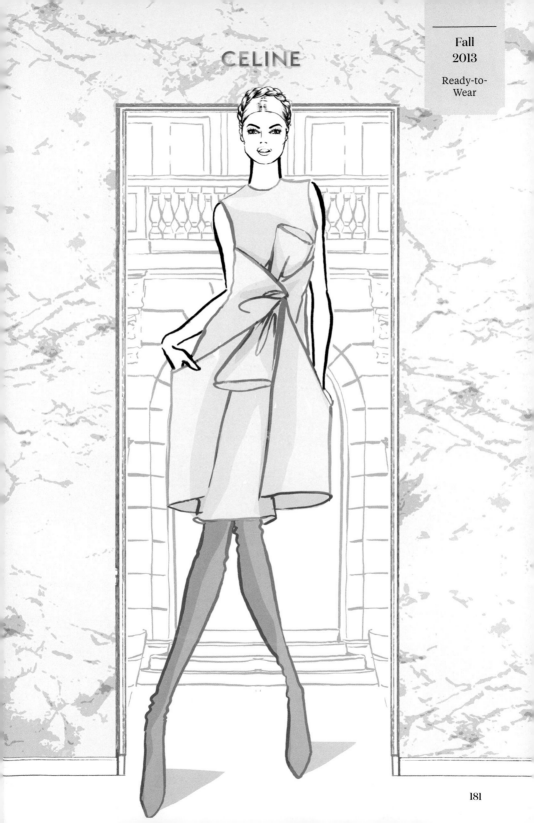

CELINE

CELINE

CELINE

CELINE

CELINE

Acknowledgements

To Arwen Summers, our second book together – thank you for making the process so enjoyable. My only regret is that we didn't have all our meetings in Paris!

To Emily Hart, thank you for once again editing this book to perfection. Your enthusiasm for French fashion was infectious.

To Martina Granolic, you are the best curator of all that is beautiful, with so much knowledge, love and genuine passion for everything French fashion. You somehow took our ten designers and curated their entire history down to the specific looks illustrated in this book. Thank you for coming on yet another creative journey with me.

To Liz McGee, thank you for casting your laser eye over every word in this book and keeping me encouraged throughout the whole process.

To Lisa Marie Corso, whenever I think I know everything there is to know about a designer, you always discover so much more. Thank you for seeking out every interesting detail.

To Murray Batten, our sixth book together! Your talent always amazes me and never disappoints. Thank you for another incredible design.

To Justine Clay, thank you for encouraging and supporting my work from the very beginning. Your belief in my art from the very early days has led me here. I forever thank my lucky stars that we met.

To my husband, Craig, and my two children, Gwyn and Will, thank you for giving me so many reasons to love the wonderful life that I have.

About the author

Megan Hess was destined to draw. An initial career in graphic design evolved into art direction for some of the world's leading design agencies. In 2008, Hess illustrated the *New York Times* number-one selling book *Sex and the City*, written by Candace Bushnell. She has since illustrated for Dior Couture, created iconic illustrations for Cartier and Louis Vuitton in Paris, dreamed up animations for Prada and Fendi in Milan, illustrated the windows of Bergdorf Goodman in New York, and created a capsule collection of bags for Harrods of London.

Hess's signature style can also be found on her bespoke, limited-edition prints and homewares sold around the globe. Her renowned clients include Chanel, Dior, Fendi, Tiffany & Co., Saint Laurent, *Vogue*, *Harper's Bazaar*, Harrods, Cartier, Balmain, Louis Vuitton and Prada.

Megan is the author of seven bestselling books and the Global Artist in Residence for the Oetker Masterpiece Hotel Collection.

When she's not in her studio working, you'll find her in Paris, dreaming about French couture …

Visit Megan at **meganhess.com**

Published in 2019 by Hardie Grant Books,
an imprint of Hardie Grant Publishing

Hardie Grant Books (Melbourne)
Building 1, 658 Church Street
Richmond, Victoria 3121

Hardie Grant Books (London)
5th & 6th Floors
52–54 Southwark Street
London SE1 1UN

hardiegrantbooks.com

Elegance: The Beauty of French Fashion
ISBN 978 1 74379 442 5

A catalogue record for this
book is available from the
National Library of Australia

NATIONAL
LIBRARY
OF AUSTRALIA

10 9 8 7 6 5 4 3 2 1

Publisher: Arwen Summers
Project Editor: Emily Hart
Editor: Sonja Heijn
Researcher: Lisa Marie Corso
Design Manager: Jessica Lowe
Designer: Murray Batten
Production Manager: Todd Rechner
Production Coordinator: Mietta Yans

Colour reproduction by Splitting Image Colour Studio
Printed in China by Leo Paper Products LTD.